The Price of Loneliness

Richard Evans

Introduction

There was an individual that just happen to appear

So appropriate was that singular title, just as I fear

For he so chose that life; the myth to remain free

 Keep me away from all of mankind, he stated with glee

I have trouble enough, he touted with a sigh

People create all types of grief and never say Hi

I feel the time has come to be on my own

No fetters or commitments, I wish only to roam

Still this man felt such discomfort and pain

Deep in his heart, he desired new friendships to gain

Flaming swift arrows of disdain do instill

A vast void in a heart just waiting to be filled

The road can be lonely on a desolate trip

If isolation during your life looks like a path to the crypt

Oh woeful is the reflection in a mirror I see

That miserable lonely person is actually me

The poem you just read is indicative of how many lonesome people considered how the problem goes beyond their abilities and how they tend to shift responsibility to others.

Many people with this condition feel the need to simplify the emotion of loneliness by believing that the therapy for this condition can be just as simple, whereas the opposite is actually true. Loneliness is a multi-faceted and complicated phenomenon that can occur at any time or at any place. Its symptoms are not always visible, even to the person who is experiencing loneliness.

This book is based on personal observation and research about the subject of identifying and defining loneliness and outlining techniques that help reduce its effects on your mind. I have included theoretical and proven concepts of how to deal with loneliness. It will also offer the sure fire method to keep the congruency of maintaining those friendships that you cherish.

We will explore the myths of loneliness and also the dangers of this vulnerable sensation as well as understanding that we do not stand alone with dealing with this sometimes very powerful emotion. We will discover as well that differences do exist in all humans and what works for you will not always work for another person at the same time.

What is loneliness?

Loneliness is usually a complex and unpleasant emotion and is prevalent in the annals of mankind.

 There are many views and theories throughout society based on the subject of loneliness simply for the reason that there are different phases of this condition and there are very few similarities on how people are affected by it.

The reasons varied as well on how people procure their sense of loneliness, so it is difficult to pinpoint one common cure. There are a variety of medications and therapeutic remedies that have been offered as valid to treat loneliness, but that in its complexity should articulate to a lonesome individual that you should use extreme caution and general common sense when dealing with one step therapy or medicine.

Loneliness can be categorized into three distinct principles.

1) Situational loneliness arises from the situation that you are familiar with or comes up in your surroundings. These feelings dissipate as you adapt to the conditions. Some prime examples are, "I'm different from everyone else." "No sweetheart, not tonight." When you have no pet or person to help console you from the unpleasantness of a recent disappointment. When you believe that no one has time for you and you claim that the person you need makes time for everyone else but not you. You feel neglect or no trust with another person and you think they are not worthy of your needs. This occurs when you are in an unhealthy relationship as well. It is too quiet for your comfort and you are living alone.

2) Developmental loneliness is someone who is trying to balance their life between contact with others and the need to be an individual.

3) Internal loneliness comes from one's own perception of being alone regardless of their present situation.

Loneliness can occur without warning and can affect a person even on a crowded street. The mindset of all people is a collaboration of both a desire to share certain ideas that we cannot contain and a thought process that excludes even the slightest consideration of revealing what in our mind to others. There are those recesses in the hearts and minds of everyone that harbor deep secrets and embarrassing moments. As some of these ideas emerge in the mind of an individual, a type of defensive mechanism develops as a reaction of guilt. A sense to be non-comital and a practice of non-disclosure during this period of time could result in an overwhelming desire to be isolated. Psychologists and counselors do not always agree on how much of your thoughts should be released and revealed to others. If you ever read a Psychology book, you should know that there are numerous theories regarding multiple behaviors. The suggestions for help varied greatly and I can understand completely why some thoughts should never be brought into the open. It is difficult to know what direction you should seek, when dealing with loneliness.

On the other hand, a release of some frustrations and hurt feelings can be a healthy remedy when you express your exasperations to a therapist or trusted friend or counselor. Be forewarned and be ever so selective and cautious when choosing a discerning ear. There are people that might use your information for their advantage or even worse, gossip about your difficulties. This might even include a well-meaning friend. In any case, you eventually do need to open up to someone to suppress your deep-seeded inclinations of loneliness.

Loneliness includes a lack of communication and a lack of connection with other beings. In our society today, communication is a dying art form. As unrealistic as it seems, a growing population means less encounters with other individuals. People do not talk with their neighbors as they did in the past. Part of this the reason that it is a reaction to the world we live in today with all of its distrust of unknown origins. The more we learn about the problems of our ever shrinking world, the more we shun the idea of creating new friendships. The media only seems to enhance this fear of new encounters because we as a human race are fascinated by disasters and calamities. The media takes full advantage of our fascinations and actually enhances the news stories that occur across our globe. Even our local news can be greatly exaggerated in what so often can be described as making a mountain out of a molehill. As humans, we gravitate towards the sensationalism of these events, but in some of us it also increases our distrust in coming in contact with strangers.

Throughout my life, it became a clear fact that many people would only come together when emergencies or harsh conditions force or propel them to communicate. When major snowstorms come into an area, people have a tendency to rely on each other and help in pushing a neighbor or a complete stranger's car out of the snow after it becomes stuck. A pessimist would state the question, does it make them look good in helping or is there a genuine need to help others in time of need? I may be the optimist, but I believe there is still a lot of good in people for the most part in this world today and that they will help out when asked or needed. For the most part I have concluded that there is usually a certain amount of good in everyone to help good friends or even a stranger in distress. Hesitation mainly comes in when a question of safety causes consternation in an individual.

The truth of the matter is that many factors come into play when direct contact is avoided. In my observation of students over the years, I have seen an increasing and distressing trend on reliance of the electronic media, which I strongly believe is an inexcusable escape from direct communication. People using these types of devices sometimes go beyond the boundaries that they normally would not enter if they face people directly. They see the electronic age as a means for protective avoidance. Unfortunately, people can be cruel when using such devices and it only cultivates more divisiveness in our society. Our current distancing is also a result a reduction of hand-written letters since the majority of people use mass media that has an unmitigated and manufactured capacity to limit their exposure to one another. The trend is alarming and I strongly believe that we should seek educational means to teach students, young people, and yes even some adults how to reconnect with one another.

Loneliness could be construed as a collaboration of unhappiness and a quest for satisfaction whose only intention is to bring benefits to their own needs. We must once more understand that different people will not react the same way in seeking a better method to communicate with one another.

When experiencing an unpleasant or unhappy situation, some people, influenced by the negativity of the world, react by shutting others out who are only trying to reach out to them in order to aid and comfort.

Pride can also have a negative effect, in that a person in despair will try to repress or hold in those emotions that they deem unworthy of their status and dignity. There is a certain point where this can become unhealthy physically. If such thoughts are causing convulsions and stomach cramps, you should seek medical advice. Holding in such unwanted emotions could literally make you sick.

On the other hand, the lonely individual tends to suppress his emotion, hoping that someone will take notice and show pity for him or her. Others are not hampered by letting their feelings be known. In a few cases, to some individuals this could be construed as a person who does nothing but complain. The lonely person should always take into consideration how his actions affect others around him in times of tribulation. Society will for the most part, judge people who constantly deploy negative consternation even when all seems well with their being. Few, if any people like to be around whiners. The average human being enjoys being around an uplifting and joyful individual that takes careful consideration of the people around them. This comes from a deep sense of self-preservation because people understand that negativity from others can affect their own lives deeply.

Loneliness can be a reaction to inactivity. The thought processes have deemed that an active life style tends to keep depressing ideas out of the head although anger is not so easily dissuaded in this activity. Some people are physically unable to operate or function without the support of others, but these individuals should not be left alone for any long periods of time.

However, most people are physically capable of movement, which leaves very little of an excuse to be inactive outside of any confined environment, such as a house, or a local cave. To be mentally alert requires that we must exit the monotony and mental entombment that we subject ourselves in time of distrust and self-pity.

Staying in front of a television for most of your life is never a healthy situation. Mankind was meant for interaction within his own species and the benefits of exercise are extraordinary for those wishing to maintain a healthy lifestyle.

Loneliness can definitely be a result of inactivity as people substitute it for friendship. Learn to become more active in making this first step for overcoming and conquering loneliness. I cannot emphasize this enough for your well-being as well maintaining your mental stability.

The Theory of the Separation Anxiety Syndrome

Retaining from my own memories as a child and observing numerous other examples, I have developed my own theory on how loneliness extends beyond the child's early age and into adulthood.

Loneliness, in a mild form I believe begins and develops in a human as a child that uses certain mental capacities as a defense mechanism when parted from familiar faces such as a parent. This does not happen in all children, but many are wary of new people that come into or are suddenly thrust into their lives. They cope with the situation by using a familiar person as a refuge when they feel threatened or discomfort. Any child has insecurities of one type or another and most of them react by bonding or having contact with someone that represents safety. Unfortunately there are those times when harsh circumstances prevail that a child must seek a refuge. Hopefully there is someone that is always there to be that comforting factor. Stress affects every living creature on this planet, but it is especially prevalent in humans whose cerebral functioning often goes well beyond a current unpleasant situation.

Loneliness can be brought on as a reaction to a trauma from a swift and self-induced terror brought on by the unknown factors. Think about the first time you saw a movie that had a scary plot or you became separated from a loved one in a crowded and large location.

 Loneliness is much like a child in a store that wants to temporarily explore those items that does not interest his adult supervisor or parent. In finding his chosen spot, such as the toy aisle, he begins to wonder if he has strayed too far from the safety of the parent, even though he has found what he wants. He is torn between staying with the toys and seeking the safety of being by his parent's side, believing that he will lose the opportunity of being where he really wants to be forever. Being lonesome is like seeking the approval of others, but debating the complexities and motives of continuing by playing it safe.

When a parent is not near or gone, children often regress into shyness, thus creating a sense of loneliness when facing uncertainty in the absence of a trusted face. Some children, for some unknown reason are receptive to meeting new people and can be very trusting and loving.

I believe however those reclusive thoughts are inclusive to everyone at certain times and develop at different levels. Some children are quite capable of developing a method to move quickly away from these mainstream tendencies more than others. Again I must stress that there are different stages of maturity and not everyone develops in a standardized fashion. Just as true is the fact that there is not a consistency in time or age that adheres to this theory. People are quite different from one another and there will never be one universal criterion that fits everyone.

This syndrome and desire for certain unknown reason goes well past adolescence with some individuals and goes well into adulthood. This bout into loneliness advances towards more prominent and progressive, although unintentional forms of loneliness. Maturity usually dissipates this syndrome, but for some it permeates their mind and takes an immense and unintended duration to disappear. People are different from each other and their emotions deviate just as much. One should not judge too quickly the people who do not develop socially as swift as they do.

In my own experience, shyness was enhanced on the first day of school. In my mind, a sudden separation from my parents on the first day of kindergarten was a terrifying experience. Crying did not alleviate my concerns, but time and patience did. Although I improved slightly my social skills with the following advancement of grades but I still carried the insecurity of loneliness and shyness well into my early high school years.

Family values and social status certainly have an impact on how we react to others. I believe that our upbringing has much to do of how we respond to the world. I was constantly taught not to go up to complete strangers, which is sensible advice, but it does limit the trust in new situations. In a normal atmosphere a child eventually develops a sense of independence for brief periods of time and may use that act of bravery to explore new and fascinating encounters.

Children love to explore the toy aisle in a store, but that may mean a brief separation from Mom. Some adapt quickly to new changes, but some children regress into a new sense of inadequacy.

We human beings were born with and given a safety mechanism. It has a two way purpose that incorporates good and bad consequences. One is the fact that it often keeps us from unsafe situations, but it also limits our encounters with new people, regardless that it does keep children from going up to complete strangers that could do them potential harm.

Some people never completely get over their distrust of uncertain situations even as they grow into their middle and high school years. There are even a rare few individuals that hang onto their bashfulness well into their adulthood. With some people it even carries over into the latter years as interests change from person to person. This does not mean that they are not normal. They should however find the right direction that will lead away from discomfort with others.

The Theory of the Immense Diversity of Interests

Many recluses believe that there is no one nearby or in their immediate area that has a common interest with them because there are too many options available in our society today. They are under the false assumption that no one can remotely come close to expressing any similar pursuits that they like, and some even have the fabricated notion that no one will like what they like. They hold on to this belief because they do not know where to go or where to begin because there are too many directions and individuals that offers activities that the individual cannot participate in or enjoy. They hold fast to the belief that people with similar interests and hobbies are remote and far away from their area. This has no basis in fact unless you live in an extreme remote area of the world. Whatever guides our personalities, some people have stronger inhibitors than others around them. Again necessity dictates that we have some communication with others in order to operate successfully in life.

**The Theory of an Over-Aggressive Ascendency and
Dominant Relational Syndrome**

Although halfway factual, this theory is based solely on the
premise that we inherit our personality from our parents or
other relatives through bloodlines. If your father has an
extroverted personality, you will acquire the same traits. The
fact of the matter is that many offspring develop completely
different personality traits from their parents. They learn
much about moral and safety issues in their upbringing, but
social instincts take on some unexpected twists and turns,
and are very often contrary to their parents' expectations.
This combination of a parent's influence and social
interactions with current and future friendships contradicts
this theory as a complete solution for why we are lonely or
not lonely.

The Recessive Inherence Genes Syndrome

Again this hypothesis rests on the assumption that shyness is included in what our parents passed on to us through their gene structure. Personality traits such as love, hate, shyness, dominating display and gender interests are basically learned. People who proclaim that these traits are only contributed through the genealogy of their parents have very little basis of fact to support their conclusions.

The Theory of an Overcrowded Society Syndrome

This theory is believed to be the closest in truth because it operates on the premise that in an overcrowded society, people keep more to themselves and avoid as much contact with their neighbors as possible. A point in fact is that when the country was being developed, people depended on their closest neighbors, which may have lived many yards or miles from them. Communication was desired much more for a culture where miles separated people longing for news of the outside world. Friendships in many ways were made stronger in the development of our country because of distances. People were more willing to invite complete strangers into their homes.

People today do not depend on people living near by as much as they use to in the past. This is true and beyond that trend of thought is the mere fact that people are less trusting of people than they were in the past.

The Theory of Emphasized Avoidance Conditioning Influence

We are taught early in life to avoid strangers. There are few of us that do not remember the emphasis that was teaching us through the media, the educational system, and through our guardians how to avoid certain individuals that we encountered for the first time or maybe even see briefly each day, such as the mailman. Conditions of society have changed radically where certain rules of safety are emphasized on a regular basis to our youngsters and seniors in a world where there are some that try to take advantage of the young and the helpless. It is an escalating problem as our world grows smaller with new and faster ways of communication.

Other trends of consideration of how loneliness operates within a society

There is the view that some individuals take of the avoidance of new ideas and a new person acquaintance because loneliness could be associated with the reluctance of taking on new encounters that involves uncertainty about the outcome. Many misguided so-called experts insist in earnest that no one should be pre-judged and that we should negate our instincts completely. Prejudice does have its very negative outcome if the thoughts prevail against someone who should not be made the focus of being shunned because of color, natural disabilities, religious affiliations, or gender. Behavior is something else altogether. Too often in today's society, deviant behavior is excused because certain individuals were not taught respect for their elders after initiating psychological and physical trauma in another person's life. If anyone has been hurt in a close relationship, there is always the strong possibility that they would have second thoughts about entering a new relationship. However many misinformed individuals would label this as being prejudice. They simply do not take into consideration that people should learn from earlier experiences. Instinct still has a high regard in my position when meeting others for the first time.

 Just about everyone in the world today had some type of a bad relationship fallout and it should be advisable to slowly pick up your life and try again, but some prefer to let one bad experience be the standard for the rest of their life because they believe in bad advice.

In trying to establish a new friendship I offer some recommendations to strongly consider.

As stated previously, safety is an inherence factor in people. We just need to learn discernment for different areas of our lives. Pre-judgment is not always bad, although many experts advise us not to be judgmental in an initial encounter with someone. Instinct at times can serve us very well. Being cognizant of the world around us can be used as a safety measure. The rule of thumb should be, to thy own self be true. Time is a good shield from becoming involved with an untrustworthy and potentially dangerous relationship. In no way does this advice mean that you should avoid others for the rest of your life, just don't be so anxious to get back on the horse right away. Be mentally prepared before you are ready to create new friendships.

The phrase; it takes two to tangle, is quite precise as an antidote for pursuing a new relationship. Many people go into a new friendship, thinking only how it will benefit them. It is vital to remember that a new friendship is not all about you nor is it a one way relationship.

A good friendship is not about taking advantage of others solely for the purpose of benefitting one person. We must be careful how we handle a relationship that we want to hold unto and keep. As human beings, we often have difficulty maintaining a fine line between being over-bearing and being sensitive to the needs of others. We must always consider the thoughts and desires of others and how our actions affect their perception of us.

In dealing with friends or potential friends, we should learn to interact with each other with common expectations throughout our lifetime. Be fully aware and know your own limitations, but expect others to respect those limitations as well.

In the same manner, respect the value of others and do not be over-zealous in your emotions. A common rule of sense is high pressure despises friends. The chemistry will not always be a good mixture for everyone you meet nor should you always expect it to work out that way. Friendships often come in small bundles that do not include the entire laboratory.

Do not try to manipulate a person who seems unable to mirror your image. Do not try to compete with a person's strengths and interest of what it is all about when you have no knowledge of what they are talking about with their chosen subject. Be yourself and be truthful. Lying to someone about your expertise in their field is a potential for disaster. Do not try to impress a skier with your prowess of skiing if you have never skied before in your life. Makeshift operations should never be unauthenticated. Remember your thoughts are not always their thoughts.

Suggestions of venturing out into the world

There is not a direction in our society today where we cannot turn and there exists an activity or a person that you cannot interact with for the mere fact that they are available somewhere nearby. Check the library or the internet for clubs or affiliations that offer an activity that you would be interested in attending. There are various musical and entertainment possibilities within your realm. Do not limit yourself with television or books.

We are ambassadors among our own kind and we can choose to be aloof and secretive or we can greet each other with a kind word or friendly greeting. A smile cost nothing, but it enhances and enriches the ones who receive it. Try it at your earliest convenience in your life. You will be surprised at how much joy it brings to those you encounter. Some people just naturally grin when coming across others and it becomes contagious rather quickly.

Remember there are thousands upon thousands of options on a planet that has billions of human inhabitants on it. You fit in the puzzle somewhere and it will not be complete without your participation.

Check into clubs, volunteer work, recreation centers that incorporates various workouts and plans and get out of your comfort zone (and away from the television.) Try to take a daily walk just to see new faces and take time to study people and take notice and see the differences in individuals. If you like a certain type of music, there is always a wide variety of musical social groups that you can participate with and enjoy. I made a point to mention this once before, but it bears repeating for the importance and the positive difference that it could make in your current life.

For the most part our fellow human beings enjoy sharing their hobbies and pursuits with other people if someone just show an interest. If someone shares a common ground with you, the ensuing conversation should naturally flow. If however the person you want to converse with shows no common comparative dialogue with you, you should still be courteous enough to listen to what they consider important. Learn to tolerate each other up to a certain point if the conversation is unlively and boring.

There will be individuals who will not reveal their likes and dislikes because they process an inner apprehension that other people will either grow bored with the subject or that they will be judged for their interests. My father made it a point in expressing interest in a business associate's hobbies for two reasons. It brought prestige and honor to him in making sales, but more important, it made the people that he encountered with this approach feel that they had more dignity and pride because someone was willing to listen to what made their life special. This kind of approach was often remunerated tenfold in response.

I worked with many young people who would be quite candid and wanted to share what they like in music or television shows. To tell the truth, I never heard of 90% of the groups that they thought were important to them. I generally did not share their particular taste in what they prefer, but I have learned to listen to what concerns them the most. When I listen, they tend to open up more about their studies and feelings. It is important to know that very few people who will not share what interests them the most if you are inattentive.

Sometimes if you are a good listener, a person will open up more to you. Strangers sometimes reveal their life stories or even at times some intimate details. I worked as a photographer with a man who played Santa Claus like a pro. You would not believe how many people compared him to a great counselor or psychiatrist because of his gentle nature. There were times however that confidential information spilled over that should not have been shared. In listening to people who open up to you, be aware of emotional values that can be sensitive and be a good listener when it is appropriate to hear what you need to hear or not need to hear at all. Sometimes if you one of those individuals that people just want to open up to, be prudent in how you handle their openness.

Bear in mind that confidentiality is a rare treasure that helps you retain friendships. Consider the fact that we often tread on thin rice paper when dealing with other human beings and their emotions, but remain wise and patient and learn to extract out slowly what should become a good relationship.

Remember every situation in meeting a new person should be generally handled differently. Young people should be greeted differently than how we greet older people. An example would be a co-worker versus the corporate boss, the president versus the lady of the household, or a man versus a woman. I must reiterate; be aware of what people expect out of you for being a friend and make sure that it will not lead to anything else besides their friendship. Remember that expectations of different people are not always going to be the same, and that would pertain to most encounters.

Avoidance of unsafe behaviors

Sadly, our world does not consist entirely of saintly individuals. Society overall has changed dramatically over the years. History unfortunately does not teach the common person that it will repeat, because many do not heed this lesson. When encountering a new individual, we must keep in mind the lesson of the past that a stranger is still a stranger without the benefit of time. You should take heed in some simple guidelines in your approach when dealing with a new person that suddenly and is not anticipated comes into your life. There have been some successful relationships that have been maintained built out of an auspicious beginning, but I want to again emphasize that you should make time a prominent factor in starting any relationship.

Times to avoid encounters with other people

The probability is huge that sometime during your life, you will encounter a person or a group of people that want to cause harm to others, whether it be physically or mentally. Considering how many individuals cross your path each day is phenomenal and the odds are that they are not all what they seem to be. I want to share some simple guidelines that are advisable in a situation that seems unpredictable or unsafe. Instinctively, we tend to view others first before judging ourselves, but it may not just be about the other person. You could be the reason for an unsafe friendship.

 If you are a danger to others, seek help or learn to calmly evaluate your feelings. Mental instability is a condition that must be taken seriously for it affects not only you, but many people around you. Consider your stress level when you are in a position to make a rational choice, usually away from the person you believe was the cause of your discomfort.

Watch for extreme groups. Your status of being lonesome or not should not be dictated by other individuals besides yourself. Let me reemphasize this point. You have the ability as a human being to make wise choices without others telling you who you should be friends with or what group you should join. There are always alternatives if you feel threatened or unwanted by someone or a group that want to live your life for you. There is someone out there just for you that does not want control to be a major factor.

A very wise proverb states; the foolish walk with the foolish, the wise person walks among those with wisdom. Use your common sense and your instincts. Adapt with whom you may, but do not associate with hurtful and manipulating individuals. There is a story involving a conservative couple in New England that wanted to contribute more to their community. They decided to host a club that was labeled in a newspaper ad as, *The Salem Chapter of Historical Preservation*. They soon learned to their dismay that the group was nothing more than individuals who practice witchcraft. Beware of manipulating and deceitful trends in the marketing of the values of the world. There are many out there who would like nothing more than ensnare your time and your money and they will use pure trickery to do just what they believe will work on you.

Exercise sensible caution and do not be an extreme radical when you join a new group. Adhere to a standard social protocol that seems to be in the mainstream of their discussions and adjust accordingly and go by their norms and rules. In short, don't be a nuisance. Drawing attention to yourself without being called upon could be a quick way for others in the group to judge you harshly.

There are definitely times when isolation could be a prerequisite because of social norms. Most people know that you do not go up to a complete stranger in New York City and ask to be a buddy. An example of this rule cites what Crocodile Dundee did by exhibiting a mainstream social blunder although with good intentions with his first encounter in the streets of New York City. He was in a taxi cab and rolled down his window and tried to make a social appointment with a man standing on a crowded sidewalk. Be practical and know that there are places it is probably better not to try meeting new people.

As you gain in prominence making new friends, try not to be the consistent social butterfly. Take time for yourself. There is such a thing as social burnout if you are out making new acquaintances constantly. You could just wind up making too many commitments.

Use your mind when you use your instincts. Some people will rub you wrong after your first encounter with them. They might be trying to impress you. Take your initial encounter with these individuals with a grain of salt when it seems to be going in an awkward direction, use that experience to improve the next encounter. Likewise it is recommended that you avoid certain and inexplicit expressions in a new personal contact. Understandably there are those individuals who take advantage and indulge in such unscrupulous participations at the expense of others. Many constantly have a knack state for stating inappropriate opinions on media, therefore creating a much unpleasant or even a dangerous situation. These postings could result in hurt feelings within individuals. If you indulge in these types of activities, be advised that what is good for the goose is also good for the gander. In dealing with people in the social media, let them understand on what opinion you have, but do it tactfully.

The world is changing and communication is changing with it.

As I have stated before, people do not have to face people directly to communicate and therefore it makes it easier to degrade another human being.

There will always be those individuals, who are nervous around other people, but there could be a benefit to this anxiety. Your cerebral cortex could be trying to enhance either your safety levels or trying to stimulate and enhance your thought processes and equipping you with the gumption to take that next step. It is as if it is trying to communicate to you, go forward and contact someone new in your life. Life is a learning process and at certain points in our lives we most grow and adapt positively to our anxieties. It may sound like a contradiction, but be wary and use common logic if a situation appears to be unsafe, such as jumping at the wrong opportunity. Do not be so impatient for companionship that you use desperate means to find a friend. Do not take on as a friend or someone who tends to always see the faults in others and loves to talk about these presumable faults to you. In my own personal view and through some unpleasant personal experiences, gossips are usually a malignant force on society and they have a tendency to cause more friction than kindness and understanding. The discussion of finances or money immediately after introductions could be a sure danger sign and should alert you to possible fraud.

In our life, we sometimes take unsafe alternatives to be accepted and loved. I knew of a few acquaintances that became deeply involved with an unsuitable person because of the lack of self-esteem or giving into the myth that no one else will accept me. Never get romantically involved with a married person. Dating a married person leads to heartache for many people, even children, who are often the innocent victims of such a relationship. The typical excuse is "I didn't know", or "He told me that he is leaving his wife." Wisdom forsakes those who rely on the wrongdoer to make the decisions for them. Don't fall into this trap.

Take quality time to really get to know a person that you believe would make a good mate for a lifetime. Compare common interests and invest time to knowing a person. The true facts will eventually come out in the positive or the negative regards.

Do not play the game of becoming the hobby of another person interests. Be truthful about yourself and what you like to do. Trying to manipulate someone in believing you know as much about his or her strengths when you have no idea what you are talking about could lead to an embarrassing interlude or even worse major heartbreak. Always be yourself and do not be about being able to play golf to a golfer if you have never played it.

In learning about what the newcomer is all about, be natural and try to compliment someone with sincerity about their interests and hobbies. Let them have their pride in the telling of their pastimes and do not ever belittle their interests if you have no first-hand knowledge.

Be aware that in your life, you will soon be near people that repel you, but find out what you can. It is possible that your first judgments can be flawed, but keep your guard up if you feel threatened by the new situation. A great idea would be to never ride on a motorcycle with a person that disregards the helmet laws of the state.

Consider the following; your attitudes could change as well the more you advance into life.

People with outgoing personalities present an interesting paradox. It is a noble gesture to be friends with everyone and some people have a knack for doing so and have a knack for being admired by many, but choose wisely and take your time to get to know someone. The first rule of thumb is to be a friend first and always and see when the friendship takes hold. Be prudent in some ways. Again all initial encounters require different approaches. We do not always make best first impressions, but being human means to have second chances and learn from our mistakes. Remember that the use of time is vital and maybe the main key in becoming more acquainted with an unknown individual. No one is invincible in keeping a false face forever. Eventually a person's faults or undesirable attributes will come to light. In maintaining a life time commitment, patience is a virtue.

I do believe that spotting those individuals with varying personalities is easy to recognize in any and all educational situations. For example, as a trained educator, I can tell immediately when some students are not engaged and are quiet when in a classroom situation.

In dealing with students, remember that they all have a need to recognize individuals for good achievements. Do not heap empty praise upon people, but acknowledge even the smallest accomplishments in individuals when it is deserved. A kind word from you could make a world of difference in a person's day.

Likewise it is sometimes simple to recognize those students who are more creative. It often depends if they are the noisy student or the quiet student. In my work I have been able to distinguish and ascertain to some extent how creative students can be identified.

Students with low self-esteem usually have less creative standards and are boisterous and crave attention and do a lot to gain it, whereas creative students, for the most part, are reserved and fairly passive and quiet in a classroom setting. Generally this is the case, but this scenario is not set in stone and there is no concrete proof to verify it. I have seen a great change in many students as they gain maturity.

My observations have led me to believe that many quiet and shy students have many ideas and are quite creative, whereas noisy students (I said noisy, not social, there is a difference) do not possess the faculties overall to orchestrate ideas comparable to their quiet colleagues. My theory is based on the reasoning that quiet students are constantly thinking about the next step in any process. Sometimes it is hard to clearly think about a process and babble at the same time. Multi-tasking does not engage itself with rational thinking for many young individuals, but changes in the thought process can evolve quickly. It is obtained through education and logical reasoning, based on quiet contemplation. What has this entire theoretical posturing have to do with loneliness? Quiet students can develop a sense of isolation if their creative side prevents them from sharing. They also believe that rules will be broken if they share in a situation such as school. Any breech of protocol is unacceptable if they have been taught not to be aggressive in school.

As lonesome as lonesome could be!

If I were ever to gamble on a sure bet, I would place a high wager that at least 99.7% of all the people in the world today could relate to that anecdote at least one time during their lifetime. It is very likely if you have not been experiencing an extreme form of loneliness earlier or currently during your life, it will probably occur later on. There are many levels and intensities of loneliness. Some people might even have the realization that they are beginning to experience or on the verge of loneliness. A dissipating party may finally lead to a person to slowly comprehending that his friends are gone. The added problem is that you have to clean up the mess.

Loneliness could come up suddenly or ever so slowly creep into your cortex. A person in a strange new environment may suddenly become aware of his situation.

Another often used phrase, No man is an island, refers to the mere fact that everyone needs to interact with another human being in the course of their lifetime. People who are marooned alone on an island were prone to depression, anguish, and in some cases became delusional and insane because of the lack of human interaction. Despite the harshness that incurs in the realm of human existence, people need to seek out compassion and be occasionally touched from other individuals. This need is an inborn trait that is prevalent at birth and continues throughout life. This is an intrinsic and instinctive trait that most living creatures desire and need to survive, because it makes us aware that we need other living human beings in our life. It is an emotion that is essential to the well-being of mankind. There is a distinct purpose of the brain in that it provides a psychological mechanism meant to stimulate a motivator in an individual to seek social connection. Loneliness does serve its purpose however in as much as it is one of these stimulators and it does serves as a motivator for a change.

But in a world that also dwells on selfishness and stubbornness, many individuals cling to the far flung conclusion that they do not need anyone else in their life. They are under the delusion that they are better off without their fellow men. Usually these are the people who secretly want the most out of their fellowmen. This is a paradox for many individuals for how many times that they believe they are on a single island in a sea of humanity. As such loneliness can even be felt when surrounded by other people. People around these individuals are just like the waves of the ocean trying to work their way around an unknown obstacle, trying to avoid the lonely outpost. Eventually the waves recede and head back into the vast network of water, without staying around to see what the island was really like.

Many see loneliness as a type of confinement where there is no hope or escape. It is somehow developed into their consciousness and comprehension that their present situation cannot be altered. They do not understand that every emotion can be overcome, but we need help to do it. Seek outside help if your feelings are overwhelming, but seek the help that is beneficial.

There are those times (and let's be honest) that the media can feel intrusive to us as individuals. Remember our previous election. Even when they try to convince us of changing our style and pattern of how we perceive as living, their endless rhetoric can have an immense impact because of the constant bombardment of their influence. You must have this; you must have that to be a better person. The vicious cycle seems endless as they constantly try to change who we really are and who we should be. Do not become the prey of other men's disasters and shady deals. We were all given a brain, but many people have a knack for shutting off the best parts of the cerebral system. Engage that part of your brain that focuses on perseverance of living a life free of harmful distractions. Regard questionable tricksters with a grain of salt and be patience with their advice. Rash decisions compel us to make bad choices.

What can truthfully be articulated about a person who tries to use his influence on you is the inconsistency of his or her claims? What is more confusing is how they never maintain a particular stance. One week they inform you to be a strong individual, the next that you must conform to a certain crowd to be part of the now generation. Sadly that constant bombardment of propaganda often asks us to skimp on our well rounded and true principles as well. No wonder people as a whole are bewildered on what they really should be like as a human being.

In trying to figure out who they really are, people sometimes lose themselves as beautiful life forms that have strayed from the vibrant individuals that they once were before the media told them differently. Many succumb to the notion that they are nothing without the approval of people that they will never ever meet in their lifetime. The result is a feeling of inferiority and not belonging if we do not conform to someone else's make shift ideal of what it takes to be an amazing human. Their outlandish reasoning is that you cannot be loved without changing your life completely. Again you must use that part of your brain known as practical reasoning that states that you are a special person and you are the one that can decide what you can do on your own and if you really need a certain item or accept bad advice. This world of ours is constantly shifting to one trend or another, but we need to maintain the common sense that we learned as observers of the high principles that we were brought up on.

Changes are inevitable, but never give up the good that is the real you. Hold onto those memories that are blessed and meaningful and true. Someone out there will respect what you keep as the important aspect of your being.

Loneliness is not just confined to the outcasts and the individuals who live at the extreme ends of the earth, but it also exists in the middle of a busy pedestrian walk way in downtown Manhattan, or going into a packed movie theater. Loneliness is not confined to a one room apartment or desert outpost. Loneliness can pop up anywhere or at any time. Our minds are a complex and constantly processing data bank of ever changing information. Our thoughts can switch over rapidly, even before we are ready for the switch physically. An unintended and hurtful phrase can prompt the remembrance of a time of loneliness. Just remember that more than likely there was no intention to bringing up such a memory. Human beings on occasion bring up those memories that are usually stored in the recessive part of the brain, on purpose for it enhances the fond reflections of a person from the past.

Loneliness exists not because its name implies isolation from others of the human race, but it also exists in the hearts of people who feel betrayed, neglected, or abused in society, even though they are interacting with other people at that precise moment. It is a human trait based on pride that we often hide our discomfort when interacting with other human beings. It is my unmitigated opinion that the news media and corporate world have a large impact on promoting a solitary lifestyle. In emphasizing individual strength, they are constantly informing us that we can do it alone or that we do not have something that everyone else has. This promotes individuality to the point that it infiltrates the minds of many deeply. Some take it so seriously that they forgo the familiarity of other individuals in a time of real need. There should be a preparatory system for people to engage more in social encounters and it should include a discernment educational policy that helps in determining any potential detrimental advice. Way too often the public is coerced by an outside influence to focus on just the negative aspects of society. A huge percentage of our news is geared towards the pain and tragedy of our world. Unfortunately the media is not only reason that people focus on the bad news rather than the good. Humans, for some deviant and not logical reason, turned on the news to observe the suffering of others. There is some type of fascination of the bad involvement in other lives that we as humans want to constantly see and the media feeds off that desire. Does this divert our pain and lonely sorrow away from ourselves or does it increase our own discomfort?

One concept that might explain this phenomenon is the fact that to a certain degree, humans process an inert sense of greed. This thought process varies greatly in different individuals. Upbringing and education play a major role in the determination of the validation of curtailing the greed in a person. In some strange way, greed employs the discomfort of others to satisfy its own needs and desires. We must remember that we have major wants and desires for the necessities of life, but we should remain prudent in how far those desires should take us. We must ask ourselves, "When do true needs become greed and just plain wants?"

Loneliness could also be contrived as a cry for attention as a response to frustration of seeing other people gaining merit for their deeds. A person reacts by drawing into a shell trying to elicit a response from others.

My theory is that we channel our emotions away from those influences that hinder our positive thoughts about others and ourselves. In a very real way, we are being manipulated day in and day out in the belief that we are all headed to a hopeless end without any indication of maintaining that hope. We need to realize that hope is always there regardless of the views that the pessimists of the world throw our way. There are always alternative pathways to consider and if that means to go at your problem from another viewpoint, then consider the possibility in a positive way.

Hurts and sorrows too often accompany the feelings of being ostracized and rejected. In some cases, the long road to recovery never ends because of all the changes that happen in the course of a lifetime. Different people we encounter affect us in different ways. A lifetime will make an opportunity for a pleasant encounter with someone we don't even know yet. It is unconceivable that we will not meet a positive person during our life. This however refers to an extremely rare person that has such a great impact on our life.

On the other hand, quite the contrary can occur. Despite the negativity that exists in many regions of our lives, we can bank on the hope that life can change at any moment.

A feeling of loneliness can disappear in a few hours, or even a day. Many people have different and varying ways of dealing with solitude and loneliness. There is not one particular protocol that works for everyone, but there are some strong major probabilities. Some solutions might surprise you. Surprisingly, one solution might even be spending time alone and giving your mind the chance to heal without the distractions that a busy world can bring into your life. This time may be used to clear your mind and develop a better solution than what you tried in the past. Rest and sleep may make the outcome much brighter the following day.

Another analogy is that loneliness is not unlike an imaginary fabric that is constantly intertwined in our mind and is an integral part of our lives. It is woven into every being life without exception, but it involves diverse patterns and colors at different times to different people. Do not take this feeling lightly for we are complex living beings with complex minds. It will happen for we are creatures of emotions and those sensations include solitary extremes. Each pattern of loneliness takes on a different meaning for each individual although at certain times people experience similar emotional stress as a result of being lonely. Overall, loneliness comes only to one person and the mesh of that fabric he has created in his own being cannot be experienced by another human.

Someone else may be undergoing loneliness at the same time that you are, but in all likelihood they occur at different levels, even for different reasons. That however does not mean that their feelings are diminished to a lower level or are more important than what you are going through. The severity of their feelings could be much worse. In any case, loneliness can be a vivid reminder of a complicity of a fabric as it can be experienced in many different ways.

If you are ever overwhelmed by your feelings, seek professional help in the form of a psychologist or counselor, even a minister.

Causes of loneliness and the reasons of why it happens

As I have stated before the causes and types of loneliness vary greatly within the sphere of human emotions. The reasons for such an emotion can be brought on by the death of a loved one, the remembrance of a friend that lives far away, or even a momentary reflection process that involves a brief encounter or flashback of a living situation, such as a home where you were quite comfortable, but had to move away from in a time of need or distress. It could stem from an unfamiliar setting or sitting by yourself in a room at your house. It occurs mainly because of a remembrance of an occurrence from your past.

Loneliness abounds with memories and the rule of thumb is that you cannot miss something unless you have experienced it at least one time in your lifetime.

There are many types of loneliness that could be included with those that were described above can also be seen as causes of loneliness. If you are experiencing any of these symptoms of isolation, consider whether any of the following events have also taken place recently in your life.

- You've recently moved away from close friends or family.
- You recently lost a friend or a loved one.
- You made the switch to living alone after living with roommates.
- You're having difficulties with meeting new people due to access issues. This could include financial problems or physical limitations.
- You've been in poor physical or mental health.
- You've avoided social situations because you fear being rejected.
- You've recently retired, quit your job or lost your job.
- You're living in a country where they do not speak your native language or you're experiencing another form of culture shock.
- You live in an area that is geographically cut off from the rest of the world.
- You've been spending an inordinate amount of time on social media. More and more studies show the links between social media and isolation. This should be a no-brainer.

REFLECTIONS OF LONELINESS

 I reflect many times about the moments that my life could have turned in one direction or the other. There was a time in my life I was so insecure that I dared not even look up at people driving cars coming towards me as I walked down the sidewalk. My shyness affected me all the way through Junior High and most of High School. It was not until my senior year in high school that I found out that other people wanted to know me better, but it did not happen until I made the first steps to communicate with others that I truly wanted to move towards to know better.

At the time it felt difficult, but actually relating to others became easy as I eventually obtained the hang of it, but taking that first step made me realize that I had to take certain risks and actions to build up my fortitude and to be accepted to others.

A prime example of my adjustment away from loneliness came out in my memories of my life after my two-year college when I had no friends around because they remained in school. I had just graduated from a junior college in Kansas and came home to a different life than what I had been used to in the past two years. It was seriously a period in my life that I was forced to look hard at my own life. I was disillusioned at my future prospects for I only had an Associate's degree. It was during this period of time that I made some unwise decisions, but it helped me to approach life differently. As hard as it is to accept this fact, loneliness is a self-inducement as prognoses in most cases.

In my own personal experience, I encountered immense loneliness at a time that I should have been able to partake and enjoyed the pinnacle of having my friends around me in a supporting role.

 In my post junior college years, I did very little to improve my social status although I constantly felt all the pangs of loneliness. I went through my 21st birthday by going all by myself to a public swimming pool.

Very few people at the age of 21 could possibly say that it was the loneliest time of their life, but I can truly say this was the case for me. Junior college was behind me and I left behind many good friends behind in another state. It was difficult to readjust to an inactive life when I came home to Colorado. Many of my friends were still in college and I had very few people my age that I could associate with at that time. It was a very lonely environment for me after I had just been through the active and rigorous life of college. I had no idea where I wanted to go and it made no sense to move on into education if I had no purpose for being there. I stayed inside a lot and my expectations were primarily unrealistic. Relying on what I had read in books and saw in the movies, I expected Miss Right to show up at my house at any time. This never happened of course. I held on to the misconception that people would flock to see me.

I dated the only available young woman at church believing that it was meant to be, but we were never equally matched. We separated after a brief engagement and that is when I decided to go out into the world and change my stationary mode of thought. It was a time for action and I made better choices. I changed churches and became part of a singles group. Opportunities opened up for me, but I still had some surprises in store for me. Spurred on by my broken engagement, I was more cautious about whom I would date. I was just glad to make new friends. I had fun with the numerous activities I had become involved with, but none of the young ladies through this group were what I needed in my life.

I tried to date a girl that was involved with another man, which quickly led to another painful encounter. I finally met my soul mate when the church group I attended combined with another church group. Life did improve tremendously for me even there were those times I thought the bad and lonely times would never change.

I learned and I suggest that you look for positive outcomes yet to be experienced. The sun does shines eventually. You should not miss the opportunities.

Who is affected by Loneliness?

Loneliness is not confined to one particular cause and it varies as the complexity of the emotion itself, nor does it affect only the poor or elderly. Loneliness includes many forms of social, mental, emotional and physical factors, now unfortunately it also involves technological pressure.

Many people in today's society rely heavily on social media to be a major part of their communication prowess, but it is also a device that further separates people on a personal basis. What often happens is that in relying on the social media for your primary source for keeping in contact with other people, it sometimes has the opposite effect and becomes an instrument for vindictive and hurtful isolation. People tend to be less hurtful when facing people face to face. It is much harder in the majority of encounters to harshly judge a person in a face to face encounter than in a social media network where information is often based on second hand information and bias from an another person's perspective.

Loneliness does not have to involve the absence of people in your life, loneliness can stem from the absence of a familiar environment, such as moving from a residence that you grew up in or from a state that you reminisce about quite a bit. When a person leaves an environment where fond memories abound, separation can lead to a variety of anxiety factors.

Certainly a crowded atmosphere is not a hindrance to loneliness and I believe it is much more common in a situation where it is less likely to relate to anyone in the immediate vicinity.

 It is possible to be totally alone in a crowd and it does create a different type of social pain. A crowded situation cannot always alleviate loneliness. How many people try to stop other people on the downtown sidewalks of New York City in order to just initiate a friendly chat or to find a new friend? People for the most part would try to avoid that individual seeking a friend out on the street. There is a proper time and place for certain encounters and I am not trying to discourage this action, but I believe the success of the attempt would result in a minimal gain. Be prudent and wise in certain settings.

There are definitely some benefits for being lonesome for a limited time. It is not always a bad psychological hindrance. Besides being a motivator for change, it also serves a person to be wary of overly aggressive figures in your life. Many people balk at the instincts of a human, but I believe that this safety factor was put into us for a reason. Loneliness could be an outlet of a protective shielding that is embedded into our mental capacity. Avoidance interacts with loneliness when a perceived (or very real) threat to our security occurs. Loneliness is a very powerful factor in the determination of what is right and what is wrong for us, but remember, any open emotion can be unreliable and fallible for we are only human. Time should always be put into play and be a key factor in the determination of a true friendship. Again this is the norm, but in some cases you could develop a friendship right away or you hit it off almost immediately. It does happen, but these relationships are rare, but instincts must be employed to a certain point. Be wise and prudent.

One of my father's hard luck stories was about a young man that my dad put his trust into and they often went out for a friendly chat over a cup of coffee. My dad's most prized procession at that time was an accordion that he showed to everyone. It wasn't long before both the accordion and the good buddy both disappeared like the morning dew. My father was infuriated and bitter and swore the vilest of revenge if he ever got a hold of his former buddy that he had entrusted his most valuable treasure. Dad eventually took it in stride and it did not dissuade him from friendly overtures to others in the future. He claimed that this theft was the main reason that he became a salesman and not a musician. He learned however to take more time in getting to know a person, but he had a personality that made everyone like him right from the start.

Avoidance because of suspicion

Some individuals hold onto a belief that you have nothing in common with people around you. I have been to a few gatherings where I felt like I had nothing in common with anyone in attendance, but I did not let that fact keep me from talking to people. I have a bad habit of employing humor to break the ice much to the dismay of my family. Sometimes it works, but I have found out the best way to have anyone open up to me is to ask them what hobbies or interests they have. Try to listen to what people want to share and make intelligent inquires when you don't understand completely what they are trying to convey to you. Try to use meaningful and intelligent questions that will illicit pride in their knowledge because they could share it with someone. Try not to be condescending or lackluster in your response.

A person can quickly surmise if you have no interest at all, so try to invoke what knowledge you have on the subject. It might surprise you that in a large gathering you are more than likely to find someone with a common interest.

Evidence that supports human contact

It is a physical reality that human emotions require that we should feel love and human contact sometimes in our life. It has been documented and verified that Hitler's Germany and Nazi doctors invoke many inhuman experiments on different groups of people, even the youngest of victims. German doctors were ordered to experiment on many non-Germanic individuals that came under their supervision to test the superiority of the Aryan race. In a few cases, they gave nourishment and water to infants, but allowed no human contact by means of comfort and touch. The result was that the majority of these infants died without the bonding of human comfort and touch. Their conclusions verified that babies die even if they are provided with plenty of nourishment, but were given no human touch or warmth. Despite these inhuman experiments, it did prove that human beings cannot survive forever without the contact from others and there is a time that we flourish with the love that we can receive or give to one another.

Humans need a certain amount of physical contact in their lives, even a big hug from Auntie Rue who manages to squeeze the stuffing out of you. We need to be hugged and occasionally touched by a pat on the head. These are all essential in the fabric of life.

It is often said that there is an actual cry for help when the phrase, I don't need anybody right now, is uttered in a sharp response. If no help is actually needed, a person could just non-responsive or use a calmer reply and could just walk away without the sentiment. If we are truthful with ourselves, we understand that people are needed in our daily lives and that the phrase, no man is an island, has some validity and very truthful insights in how we handle stress and loneliness. In dealing with others, it is important to know you are dealing with many different types and levels of human beings.

Human are bizarre in that they essentially say things that they truly want the opposite of what they want to happen.

Individuals must realize that they do not corner the market in loneliness. It manifests itself in all types of humans, all social status including the poor and the rich, the beggar and the worker, the bad and the good, the young and the old, any male or female. No one is immune to the adverse effects of loneliness when it strikes.

It is almost impossible to be alone on this planet for the mere fact that there are very few places on solid land upon this earth not touch by man's treading mark.

It is the extremely and unbelievable individual that tried to isolate himself for a lifetime from the rest of the world. Hermits and monks must share with someone if only to strengthen their resolve of isolation.

It could be stated as well that the condition of loneliness is a means to avoid the urgency of the world's current problems and ever growing challenges of which there are many. Some people rely on the avoidance in that it is often used as an escape in coping with communicating with others that they see as inferiors or superior. This self-induced circumvention is endowed with our inner being to avoid unpleasant encounters, particularly when those encounters deal with the unknown or new experiences that we have set in our minds as apprehensive. It is difficult for some people to take on new commitments or even embrace them fully. However, sometimes the risk is worth the embracing of new ideas or friends. As human beings, we should try new encounters in order to not be stagnant in a particular state of mind.

The existence of our being is built on exploring life and the endless possibilities that it offers. We must not confine ourselves to a meager existence, but be open the possibilities that our mind wants to experience. Are there hurtful nuances and enclaves out there to avoid? Yes, most certainly, but beyond that is a whole new world to discover if only we take that one small chance.

MYTHS OF LONELINESS

Some people take it for granted that they are either immune from being lonely or that they control the feelings of others around them. There are a few misconceptions about loneliness and I tried to share some of the questions that might be foremost on your mind.

I can be selective?

 Yes and no. It takes two to make the decision. Don't believe that the decision is for you to make alone. Wait patiently, don't wreck or ruin a relationship by moving too fast.

Loneliness is just someone being stupid.

Wrong, do not, I repeat do not ever consider yourself stupid because of loneliness. Millions of people, including the most brilliant and wealthy endure the pangs of loneliness.

If I stay home, my chosen friend will come knocking at my door.

Believe this hoax only if you want to make friends with a

conniving salesman or a religious sect parishioner who only wants you to be the latest pansy for his cult.

No one out there shares my interest.

I must emphatically disagree with this concept. There are a variety of people out there that share your interest. Go and find out where they are located.

I must lower my expectations and inhibitions to find the friend that I need in my life.

Although no one is the same, don't lose your good sense as well as your abilities to make good choices. Stick to your morals and do not let anyone talk you into a situation that you deem unsafe or unwise. Experience new challenges, but find out all you can before making a wise and prudent decision. However in saying this, remember that a lot of people are out there waiting for a friend like you and they think their social status is beneath you. Help each other out if needed, but the passing of time is essential for a friendship to develop.

We will immediately and simultaneously like each other.

Possible, but very unlikely on a first encounter, nor can this condition prevail just because it is based on a feeling. Good friendships will take time and you learn more about each other. Learning is always the fun part in a budding relationship.

Common traits and misconceptions of being lonely

For a person to have loneliness occur is a sign of a cerebral
normal function, which entails thinking about how you can
improve your current situation. Loneliness is a part of
physical and mental growth which is common to everyone
who has a healthy mind. It also exists in special needs
individuals, but again it is showing developmental growth.

If loneliness is to be considered an ailment, it is an ailment
that can be corrected with self-determination with new and
past encounters. It is important that we realize that
loneliness is not a sign of weakness nor is it a brain malady.

Believe it or not loneliness is an occurrence that is common
to all of mankind. Everyone is lonely sometime during their
life and no one is immune, but many learn overcome this
condition. Every man and woman experiences loneliness at
some time in their lives, so do not hold onto the concept that
the burden of loneliness is for you alone.

We as human beings would not strive for improvement and a
newness for non-encountered experiences without
challenges to our system and way of thinking. It is a deterrent

to stagnation and endless sorrow. Loneliness does happen to anyone that has emotion at certain times, which is everyone.

It is said to never be lonely is to not have dreams or possess any type of emotion. These feelings do occur at intermittent times in our lifetime.

Think about surprises and occurrences that brought you joy and happiness in your past. Unexpected events do and shall occur for we live in a constant world of change, be it happy or sad. We must reflect on our joy as well as the painful memories. A sudden turn of events can just as likely evaporate the loneliness that resides in us.

There could be unexpected news of the birth of a child, the arrival of a new and beautiful morning or a sudden appearance of friends; an invitation to a grand event or a sought after party.

There could be a sudden revelation of something recovered or mind boggling experience, such as a movie that becomes a distraction from your loneliness or a piece of comforting music.

Unfortunately a catastrophe in the news could force you to focus more on that major problem and keep you from dwelling on yourself which brings up another poignant fact. Some of these changes we take for granted because we tend to focus on the negative aspects of our society.

We rely so much on our thoughts, our actions, our verbal words, and they all combine to display to others what we are and how we are also perceived by others. In truth we live in a judgmental society.

Our modesty is useful, but it can become a temporary burden as well. No one will judge us the same way as others do. Some might see you as obnoxious; others might see you as playful. Others might see you as a shy person with sudden perks.

As humans, we need constant exposure with different individuals which help in creating interaction that helps to induce a natural growth away from shyness.

When people come out of their reclusive nature, they overreact in an overwhelming behavior. When you come out of your reclusive shell, do not over do for it could become a major deterrent in a friendly attitude for others towards you. The key is to remember that patience is crucial. I have never liked being near an over-aggressive individual, as most people would, and I balk at the times I have been accused of it. Quite honestly I can see where some people would see that in me. In your new found enthusiasm, do not overwhelm people, for that new and unexpected behavior could be a major annoyance for them.

I have come to the conclusion that quiet people often conceive of a world in their minds that conforms to their passions that they will come up with different scenarios that passes through their minds. Some of these expectations are unobtainable, but all individuals have their unrealistic dreams, but creativity is a function of the brain that is displayed more in others, but is hidden deep in everyone.

Through personal observations during my work I have come to the conclusion that boisterous and loud students do not for the most part, process the creativity that reserved students have. The first students I first encounter are the ones who come up right away and introduce themselves, usually in an attempt to use their charm to disarm me and to gain confidence and approval for an act of disobedience that they are about to initiate. Their low self-esteem calls for attention and recognition.

For some individuals, to prolong loneliness is a choice, but it is the rare individual who has this inherence desire. As is the case for some, it is preferred because of something that they perceive as wrongful behavior that was incorrect or actually a fact that they are concealing a realistic non-conformist behavior. A point in case is the villain who rarely wants to associate with society that he had just wronged. He has a reason to shun people, but this is because of his doing.

Change itself is an integral part of our mind and life. For humans there is no perfect comparison or conclusion, for we are creatures of a vast and complex self-induced mystery.

Some lonely individuals claim that no one likes them and they refuse to adapt to other trends of thought. It is unrealistic to claim that no one else has the same likes and dislikes you have. There is always someone somewhere that shares your dislikes and same interests.

Some people display behavioral traits that mimic someone in

their life that they admire greatly. These copy-cat mannerisms are displayed by people who knows how to draw attention to themselves by displaying the acts of another and who wants to obtains that attention that the other person he or she comes into contact with for the purpose to acquire attention. I always wanted to emulate my heroes and admired figures. As a youngster I tried to be like my older cousin and I looked up to him to be my model of what I should become as a person.

A simple example could be; I want to be a football player because they always seem to gain all the attention. Don't make this your main focus in life and your ambitions. We should spread out our focus to include other variations of activities.

We must be willing to continually set up new goals and think of opportunities for improvement. This can be accomplished in many different ways and in the variation of time frames. Rush not to your ruin. Loneliness is adjustable and can dissipate if we incorporate a different state of mind.

Other Dangers associated with loneliness

A scene in the comedy movie, Airplane, shows a young man sharing his problems with anyone he sits by, thus causing great consternation each time with the second person who has been listening. There is a great deal of truth in this movie despite trying to convey humor. Most people do not want to deal with another person's problems unless they first ask to listen. Even then, minimize the input of your troubles when sharing concerns with a seemingly helpful soul. Counseling should also minimize the output of advice. Loneliness is a strong emotion. Every emotion has some benefits if held under check. Loneliness is no exception. It is an extension of our inner most desires to change our current status of our mind. In a small way it is a defense mechanism. Altering our course cannot cast loneliness completely out of our mind forever, but it is preferable to a continuation of that emotion forever.

Loneliness is not the catastrophically malady that many individuals make it out to be. It can be overcome, even though some choose to hang on to it and use as a mental clutch, but like a clutch it is meant to soften the pain and then is to be discarded as the feeling heals. The memory may linger, but life goes on and we must make strives to overcome the grief that is associated with loneliness.

Symptoms of Loneliness

If your main question is, how do I identify loneliness, you are going to discover quickly that you are trying to make the complicated a simple matter and it cannot happen. The symptoms of loneliness are not always easy to diagnose, especially in a crowd. Sometimes it is easy to distinguish who and what person is afflicted with this ailment. For many, who are observant, it is quite obvious who is lonesome.

 The symptoms that are listed below are not all good indicators of loneliness and they do not always infer that these signs of loneliness will occur simultaneously. However, the first three are very good indicators that a person is lonely.

- A mental state of mind of feeling isolated from a certain situation
- An empty feeling
- The perception of being alone
- Discrepancy of not being wanted in a desired field of interest
- No definite criteria to define or diagnose a state of clinical loneliness

- Low energy
- Sleep problems
- Loss of appetite
- Over eating
- Increased substance abuse
- Feelings of hopelessness and loss of self-worth
- Depression increases
- Anxiety increased
- More sickness than usual
- Physical aches
- Excess shopping
- Attachment to material things
- Untidiness
- Binge watching of television
- Craving warm things such as a hot bath or hot cocoa
- Checking with phone all the time
- The belief that you are being ostracized continually whether factual or not
- Abdominal tightening, prolonged depression, anxious feelings and thoughts- if these anxieties become pronounced, seek help.

Some of these symptoms can be controlled, even if your will power must come into play. Changes can be made if you put effort into your determination.

Eating too much is a by-product of loneliness and depression- both can be changed like smoking for it is a controllable factor.

Lonely people, especially the elderly buy things they don't need- get into worthless sites offering opportunities.

Loneliness causes behavior changes to a degree that occasionally cause people take on imaginary abnormalities. There are numerous hypochondriacs that go to the hospital because of a deep sense of loneliness.

Know that there will be individuals that abide in this world that will make you uncomfortable. Find the strength that exists in hope and love that helps you cope in a noble and positive way when dealing with these people that respond to others with a hard heart. In many cases you can be the instrument that softens their hearts by how you respond.

Find that gentle strength in your own heart and use it sparingly and understand their discomfort as well.

Use tact when you can. Some people may not realize that a common bond of uneasiness could be the key to draw out the personalities of both parties.

DIFFERENT THEORIES ASSOCIATED WITH LONELINESS

As much as we want to create a perfect world for ourselves, we must realize that everyone who wants their own perfect world has to contend with other individuals whose conception of a perfect world is quite different from our own concept of our perfect society. Everyone is unique and quite different especially when it comes to our mindsets. Some people just have a knack for gentleness and understanding. Some are naturally great leaders, but can be too harsh in their judgments of others. I do not know of anyone that has not encountered some type of a grumpy person in their past.

We must exist with and endure other people. No man is an island unto himself and patience is a commodity that few want, but it is essential for existing on this planet if we are to dwell among other individuals. We are born because of the intercession of other people and it was not meant that we are to exist alone. There will always be that person that will try to force their will upon others either by trickery and deceit or by their actions.

Although not foremost on our minds when we seek out connecting with people is an essential question, are we using other people for our own benefits? Our goal for the most part is self-serving and self-gratification. This is not an unreasonable goal if we understand that we must consider the feelings of the other person and take it into account. Just as the phrase, it takes two to tangle, emphasizes, we cannot expect everyone we are attracted to, to be responsive in the same manner. Think of your favorite and most beautiful movie star. If she accepted every invitation that she received, there would be no room for privacy. Always think about the other person in a developing relationship. Friendships are a great thing, but try to remember that our initial response could be conceived as intrusive by some.

If a person lacks tact when dealing with a new person, it could be a true indicator of his or her own insecurities or inability to communicate properly. It could mean that they are just as lonely as you are or have been hurt emotionally from a previous experience or relationship.

In meeting a new person, try to maintain your own encouraging way of tactfully and presenting yourself to a new person coming into your life. You will be amazed in the manner your approach people and how it will benefit you both.

Likewise we cannot selfishly expect that everyone will conform to our standards. (Politicians are great at this expectation!) Take great care in not adopting a complete mood swing quickly. Intentions or improper words without thinking can backfire and cause irreparable harm in a relationship. Ask pertinent questions.

We use a certain amount of fabrications during our existence in the use of justifications to avoid others.

If you believe that you are experiencing any type of acute clinical depression. You should check with a counselor or psychological professional. It is vital to remember that the mind performs psychological warfare on our own physical body. This is especially true with adolescents, whose mind conflicts greatly with their developing bodies.

The human mind often develops a mire of thought processes which ever so often conflicts with other thoughts that exist in the mind.

Education is the main key, essential in the development of the mind. How a child is raised is important.

A self-made man does not exist and never will for such a determined soul that hangs on to this concept only seeks havoc upon himself and others around him. Be not haughty with your successes, but humbly share your joy.

People exist with the inherence drive to be loved and to communicate with other people. We cannot do both or either alone. Whether you believe in the biblical story of creation or not, it does make sense that we were made for each other. As one mountain man said to another, "These hills have no need to move, why should I?" His partner's reply was, "Well, I'm no mountain. A man belongs to his own kind, like them or not!"

It is beyond our comprehension to scope the reasoning of why we display certain emotions at the most inconvenience times, but hopefully we learn from experiencing all we can to keep in check and not repeat deepening displeasure and loneliness. Man is an unpredictable creature. Marketing advocates have been trying for years to predict exactly how consumers will purchase certain items. It changes drastically from year to year for we are beings that grow and change and man has no way of predicting the mood swings of others.

Some markets even try to push merchandise that we don't even need.

After all we are human beings and despite what some so called experts come up with for combatting such negative emotions with therapy and pills, we are still fallible and fragile beings that subject to change. Our emotions cannot stay in one condition for a long period of time, but we are capable of employing a stabilizing factor into these feelings and can attempt to keep them in check. For the most part we must have a willingness to do so. The mind cannot stay stagnant unless it is a dead piece of tissue. Ecstatic behavior is contingent upon experiencing a lull in emotions for which we can display coming out of and enjoying life.

Constant and unchanging patterns in our cortex results in a dull and lax luster state of the mind. We should never let our minds grow stagnant. Our minds are constantly working, but sometimes the rest of our body has trouble adjusting to the continual bombardments of the thought process.

There are various reasons for loneliness, but some people purposely impose upon themselves isolation for a variety of reasons. These could involve shyness, guilt, an inability to express why you want to be left alone, anger, sorrow, believing you will not be accepted in a particular group. It was not and is not uncommon for people with different social statuses to incorporate cliques or being associated with people with a like mindset. This kind of thinking tends to limit a person from experiencing a variety of cultural and social interaction.

At certain times a good cause for isolation could include study, planning, decoding secret files, exhaustion, and sleep. Isolation is not always a negative occurrence and some people with fortitude seek isolation to express emotions without the excuse of embarrassment.

Loneliness could hinge on the intercession of another behavior, terror, sadness, regret, a sudden urge that comes in the middle of the night for no apparent reason at all or because a dream causes a lapse of confusion and fear. It is quite natural and appropriate to reflect on the important aspects of life while you are alone. Remember you are not alone when you experience these bouts of unwanted thought processes. Unwanted emotions could come because you feel you have been singled out for some unknown or personal reason. Try to take a calm approach and logically conceive of an alternative when these situations arise.

You lack a certain skill or talent that others around you have.
Be a vessel that wants to be filled with information.
Education is to be cherished and sought after your entire life.
All you need to bring is your mind. School is not the only
place to learn. Life itself is a continuation of obtaining
knowledge. Embrace technological advances and see how
they operate. Take care however in that they do not
consume your entire life. I'm still skeptical about these new
cars that operate without a driver, but my curiosity is
fascinated by seeing one in operation. I keep wondering if
these vehicles can do any better than their human
counterparts and without drivers who are fallible at certain
times that they drive.

Do not always focus on yourself, take notice of the talents
and skills of others around you and ask pertinent questions. If
you show interest in what they do, you might just receive
reciprocation from the same person. Look for those common
points of interests that will lead to a satisfying discussion.

Believe me it is not always easy to avoid a mortifying and
embarrassing situation in trying to initiate a new relationship.

When greeting people we know nothing about and such an encounter can and will happen, hopefully we learn from mistakes that we made and that is because it is a part of life. I went to a social gathering for my wife's business and of course I never previously met most of the people who were attending. One man came up to me and introduced himself and his partner. My immediate inclination was naïve and I asked the man what kind of business they were involved in, never guessing that he was talking about a personal relationship.

If a harmful encounter is imminent, learn how to avoid the situation by questioning and determine by further studies and investigation if it is something that you have not considered. In this case I kept my mouth shut and tried not to assume anything for the rest of the night. I incorporated the one simple rule of listening carefully the rest of the night before I spoke again.

Affirm the actions of others even though you do not understand it completely. We will most likely encounter people with all walks of life. There will be some very nice encounters with certain individuals, but we will have no common interests with them. If a person wants to know you better and is quite sincere in his attempt, why put aside his ideas just because you have no connection in what he is sharing with you. Give them the pride by listening or just ask questions on what you do not understand.

There are numerous examples of the paradox of conflicting interests such as a ballet opera as first seen by a blue collar worker who enjoys all-star wrestling, or a knitting grandmother who watches her first ever hockey game and she tries to explain icing to someone nearby. Learning to adapt to an unfamiliar situation should be a priority in obtaining a mature posture.

Romance versus Loneliness

Romance is desired from many, but it is a psychological nightmare for several anticipating individuals that experience the extremes in trying to provoke or enhance love in their lives. Fairy tales have convince many prospective romance seekers that love can be immediate and full of happiness forever and ever. The truth of the matter is that procuring a lifelong partner is often hard work and is sure to be painful as we juggle through the selection process. Don't let this discourage you however for we must learn that a successful relationship in intimacy will take time and sacrifice. The trick is determining who is right for you and that you understand that the road to love is strewn with bumps and detours that we would rather just ignore.

One sure fire way to end a budding romance is that egos tend to stand in the way of true love. There is the old adage that pictures don't lie, but liars take pictures. Be aware of the man or woman that constantly sings his or her own praises. I can sum up a certain personality in five words; junior egos relying on kissing stimulations. Take the first five letters of the major words and you come up with jerks.

There are many men out there that believe strongly that they are God's gift to women. People can often hide their true personalities for a while, but eventually their contemptuous and arrogant ways emerge as time advances. It should be logical to keep your distance from people who tell you what to do all the time and who you should be seen with for their convenience. Such an individual has unethical purposes for his need of controlling others. It is nice to provide for others, but maintain your lifestyle that you have comfortably set aside for yourself without the interference from others that would take advantage of your giving. Change should be gradual and well thought out.

As we enter the phase in our life when we believe that we are ready for that long time commitment, patience is often over-ridden by what we believe is the right time. The problem is that we must rely on others to go along with our plan and it does not always work out the way we want it. Ladies, I want to especially address your mindset at this time because even though norms have changed somewhat where women are more aggressive than from the past, some of you still hold onto traditional values and expect the man to be the pursuer. It is hard at times, but ladies should take a stand at certain times and say no to potential suitors that they do not want in their life. Don't ever let a man coerce you into believing that he is your only and last chance for a lasting relationship. Remember that you absolutely have the right to your own decisions and saying no should be your privilege.

I would add one more suggestion. Don't put all of one particular gender into your own psychological category. Just because you are wronged by one member of the opposite sex does not mean you will receive the same treatment from everyone of that same gender. You might just try not dating the same type of personality that you usually gravitate towards. Turning vile towards all members of the opposite sex is one of the most unappealing attributes to anyone's personality.

Even after stating that possibilities are endless in your pursuit of love and no one fully understands the psychology of the heart, there are those places that are quite inconvenient for a lasting relationship on this earth. It is quite true to look for love in all the wrong places.

There are places on this planet where loneliness could hamper your life or your future prospects. I would strongly suggest to anyone wanting a mate that is interested in a long term relationship that you should never ever start in a bar.

I will not ever advocate frequenting bars to find a romantic liaison, because frankly speaking, alcohol and loneliness are a volatile mixture. There is always a constant danger that someone will try to take advantage of your disposition if you became intoxicated. Do not become accustomed to lowering your inhibitions as well as your good senses.

We must face the facts that there are people out there that will never accept any type of responsibility for their action, even if it drastically changes the life of another person.

You do not need to jump off a cliff to know that it is a bad idea and picking up a drunk for a date is just as dangerous.

Morally this world has drastically disintegrated and mankind is constantly being manipulated and desensitized into believing more and more of adapting the standards of a gray philosophy and deserting a black and white social order.

When it comes to the subject of alcohol and romance, the majority of people in today's society tend to put on blinders on how it affects lives in a negative fashion, even though they know of a close friend or relative who went through a traumatic and emotional aftermath or had an unexpected pregnancy. Social drinking by and large is acceptable in our society and people look beyond its consequences. My suggestion is to be wary of what you do before you even consider a bar. No one expects to become fallen down and stinking drunk, but the supposedly big thrill often overcomes a logical recourse. More people should open their eyes to how much this subject is ignored.

If you might believe that these thoughts are prudish standards, then you are correct, but I am proud to maintain a lifestyle that excludes being one of the crowds that provokes problems because of their excessive life expectations. Certain realities are never outdated. Play no games with extreme or poor behavior because it is what everyone does. This statement in itself is a poor excuse to completely overturn or disrupt your life. A ruined life is not always retrievable.

I have seen too many prime examples of the effects of alcohol. My own father continually told the story how his bed kept spinning in controllably after he had consumed bourbon.

In the majority of unintended one night stand after making the local bar scene, I have come to the straightforward conclusion that drunks make easy prey. No, I can truthfully say that I have never personally encountered this situation, but there were many people that crossed my pathway in life that were involved in drinking endeavors and were on both sides of a bad limited relationship because of alcohol consumption and they regretted it for the most part. Seeking comfort and friendship in the intake of alcohol is almost like playing Russian roulette. I am amazed that people need to pose for a picture with a drink in their hand in triumph or if they scored a huge victory. Is it a status symbol or a symbol of idiocy? I cannot emphasize enough that there is a definite situation and place that should be avoided and a vast majority of these come from logical reasoning and caution.

My own personal advice because of what many had shared with me is to be one of the few and not the many. Cause a new sensation by not conceding to what is considered the norm. Be unique and try not to conform to the standards of the world that can cause unjustifiable and irreparable harm.

My suggestion is to study the individuals that frequent the bars. Watch for unusual behavior and consumption frequency.

Are they promoting themselves or the drink? Loneliness is no excuse for poor judgment at its extreme capacity. Intoxication has incapacitated many a lonely soul who believed that drinking enhances the experience of love.

Remember there are always several alternatives that are open and available to you. Do not limit your capacity for safety. Happiness and fun comes in a variety of ways and desires. Overall it makes sense to keep away from scandalous and possibly dangerous people you usually meet at bars. Everyone uses the excuse, I can handle it and everyone else does it. Remember well my cliff jumping analogy.

There is always the chance of having major misery and heartbreak after a one night stand with someone you met at the bar. Use your brain as well as your heart.

Romance can happen anywhere, but the least likely place to find it is sitting at your home. Go out and interact with others, but choose wisely where you go. Frequent the places that catch your interests and personality.

I had good friends of the female persuasion and some probably consider me to be a likely candidate for a lifelong partner, but I was cautious with one and the other one rejected me. It was better in the long run that both relationships failed for it open the door for my present beloved wife.

Love or some interest in someone could happen at first sight, but it could turn quickly to a hasty decision. Do not let this discourage you from pursuing a possible friend.

Infatuation is one thing, and love is another. Infatuation is immediate and love takes time. Love is kind and not boastful or jealous. Guidance should not only come from the heart, but from the brain as well.

It is important to take into consideration that the large majority of people will not end up with our first love. Many of us go through a variety of relationships and the ending of some of these will be psychologically painful. I can guarantee that the sun will come up tomorrow and you should chalk up a broken romance as a life experience. We are fallible humans, who expect to always find the perfect lifetime mate and it flows in everyone at least one time in their existence. Flaws exist in everyone, even the one searching for the perfect mate. Perfection is not plausible in anyone, but a seeking person should try to maintain a higher standard in their selections and don't ever date someone with obvious flaws like an abuser or one who has an excessive dominating personality. The key to remember is that we are all human beings with obvious shortcomings. The self-made man is a myth and we must maintain this concept when seeking the right person for us.

Some physical qualifications are also essential when seeking a mate. A good candidate should be a good provider and have a job. Dating a person with no ambition at all is a very likely disaster in the making. Over half of the relationships in the United States end in divorce and the main reason are the conflicts over money or indecision from a job perspective. As you dive deeper into a relationship, ask pertinent questions about their future plans and raising children or expectations for the near future. You may want things that the other person absolutely will not consider. Make it sound like you are interested in their ideas for the future, but if it is not in your plans, talk about options, possibly even the ending of the relationship. Remember that your expectations could be excessive as well. I knew a girl in college that would never marry anyone that was not a farmer. I wished her well, but I kept thinking if she might have pass up other opportunities that could have worked.

Use good judgment in extending your trust

Humans are the most contradictory manifestations for never saying what they really mean. Hopefully you will encounter the majority of individuals that have been taught a certain amount of a semblance of telling the truth in their upbringing.

Be aware of constant lies and manipulations in a potential friend. As much as people keep reminding you to not be pre-judgmental, it is quite acceptable to use caution as well.

Humans are a contradictory species and if you really want to be honest about it, can you truly say I never lied in my life. People do learn to be truthful to a point, but their minds struggle at times to maintain complete honesty, especially when confronted with poor judgment or wrong doing on their part.

An assortment of manipulations exists because of pride selfishness and stubborn shame.

Even if you were wronged or assume that you are right, learn from the experience and be aware of your own shortcomings as well. We are all imperfect and we are prone to make mistakes. The idea is to minimize what goes wrong. Be aware as well that all humans are different and that we all were created with different perks and flaws, but we must iron out our differences to peacefully exist with one another.

In meeting a new person, don't be aloof and snobbish. What you may think is an improbable friendship could change the more you interact with someone new. Most people respond favorably (if they are mature) to overtures of your wanting to learn more about them. Be a friend first and foremost. I remember well a time that just a small difference in a greeting turn my mind into the opinion that this person thought she was much better than me. Instead of a regular handshake, she curved her hand downwards into a c position and barely touched the top of my index finger in a greeting. My thoughts immediately went to, she is afraid of me, or she is showing through her actions that she is superior to me. I always expect a good strong handshake from anyone I first encounter, so her greeting was appalling to my sense of courtesy.

Whether we believe it or not, it is not always known when we have a lasting impact on others. A famous phrase states, a

rose's beauty fades and withers, but the memory of its
perfume lasts forever. Your behavior could have an
irrevocable influence on people. Be a positive force for those
you encounter.

Remember lifetime experiences may be overwhelming with
many people around you or meeting a new gathering of
individuals, such as at a party or new workers. If you are
completely uncomfortable with this type of situation or you
displayed a high degree of anxiety in this type of setting, seek
professional help.

Do not try to influence the whole world all at once. Over
confidence has been the doom of many historical figures, but
the trying made many of these figures became detrimentally
infamous.

The many benefits of solitude because an examination of priorities is not always a bad thing

Being by yourself can be a beneficial and a fantastic method to clean your mind from unwarranted distractions and give you a new perspective. Alone time allows us to gather our positive thoughts of how we can handle our next situation. The clutter of a busy world is usually not beneficial to anyone in a never ending scenario.

It gives you time to exercise the way you want without competition. A small hike or an uninterrupted workout at the local gym not only revives your physical well-being, but supports the thought process as well.

Remember if there is no clutter in your mind, it could be a time for beneficial reflection.

Try not to be the constant social butterfly. Too many people in your life make it very inconvenient when you need to take time for yourself.

Loneliness proceeding death

 Why was I allowed to set such fear upon my heart?

No one so near can share what dread keeps us apart

When will death's grip lashes out with her mighty sting

I only hope and pray when I close my eyes forever, great comfort it will bring

If only pain were only a fantasy and mere illusion

What then could I be afraid from life's final conclusion

Why must I endure without empathy or cause

No greater calamity shall haunt my soul without pause

Somewhere a lonesome and hurting soul in torment does woefully resides

This shall be my burden to encounter such agony before I too shall die

This particular chapter was especially difficult for me to express my views, not because I will face this possibility some day in the future, but because I wanted to display some empathy towards those individuals that probably are suffering from the most difficult form of loneliness. In trying to dive into the mindset of a person facing an early demise, I was compelled to create this chapter because I recently have seen too many examples that have suddenly arisen that has brought my attention in this category that frankly I cannot completely understand what these souls are going through. As I write these words, I am dealing with the loss of one of my siblings. I am continually trying to think about what her last valid thoughts might have been.

However, having to admit that fact, I do comprehend and acknowledge that in facing imminent death, the majority of these people experience loneliness in its deepest form. It is a loneliness created out of fear of the unknown and it cast doubts about the understanding of friends and relatives who will remain behind in this world.

It has amazed me the many and varied ways that people face their ultimate demise. Some are stoic and bravely announce their fate in defiance and calm demure. I cannot help but show my admiration for these people because I am almost certain I would not be able to show the same amount of courage that they have revealed to the world.

Some hold it completely in quiet reserve and silently linger until death's shadow overtakes them and they accept it peacefully. Some might even welcome death, but there had to be a time during their life that they dreaded this prospect.

Others reflect on a past that they cannot change, but wish they had in sad remorse.

There is a majority that are completely frightened by the prospect for they know not what is an uncertain future and they scorn the idea of an afterlife and come to the conclusion that dead people are nothing but a cold piece of meat.

Many lose their reason to know what is forthcoming and their memory is gone forever.

Some change instantly and turn to spiritual and soul searching guidance.

Others react in anger and spew out what is wrong with the world and mankind in general. They refuse to believe that this course was meant for them and not someone else that deserve the pain of death more than them. For many they cry out in pain and know that relief cannot be given to them in their current existence. They are overcome with emotion and wish for a speedy end. They lash out at even loved ones. Tolerance fades quickly and they are torn between being a burden, or the other option is fighting for all they are worth. It brings on a loneliness that is hard to bear.

People who have experienced near death occurrences have encountered different reactions, but I will try to illustrate the typical intersession between life and death by studying the people who have come back from this encounter.

A non-self-induced person (one who does not purposely try to take his own life) who has gained consciousness after blacking out, often describe the void as a quickening of time and an encounter of near euphoric proportions. These encounters are well documented and I have talk to many individuals that had blacked out and believe that they were near death, and they have verified this passage of time and euphoric feeling.

The self-inducing person has a completely different and horrifying experience, usually with unintentional results.

Assuming a quick peace, they often experience a delusional and horrifying result. In their black out period, they experience intense mental anguish and pain after their attempt to intentionally bring an end to their life. It is as if the mind rebelled against the body for this attempt and it made sure that there would be no pleasant transition. Again this has been well documented for failed suicide attempts that had momentarily blacked out and were near death. Loneliness can only be alleviated by the living. Do not actively seek death my friend, for when it is ready it will seek you out.

Spiritual Concepts

It is certain that people approaching death, thoughts can be excruciating and their minds are in turmoil. It maybe not painful, but the thought of leaving loved ones behind and facing an uncertain passage into the realm of the afterlife can be daunting. Whether you believe in an afterlife or not, sometime during your life, you had to consider this distinct possibility that it could exist.

We are creatures of the expansion of ideas and there have been those times in everyone's life that they did not consider, however brief, what might lie out there beyond our perception.

What compels mankind to reach beyond the stars or seek other answers just beyond his grasp? Why has man always tried to answer the essential the unobtainable and ultimate essential question? Is there more to life than what I am experiencing in my mortal body?

Men in history have always been compelled to seek a higher meaning in life. Is the possibility of an existence beyond our realm realistic?

Why consider church as a viable option for combatting loneliness if you do not believe in the Bible?

I want to justify through nine valid reasons for a person who is lonesome to consider a church as a viable option even if you have no belief in the concept of heaven or of God. Churches, for the most part are very welcoming to newcomers seeking a friendly venue of participation. If you are considering church as a possibility for meeting new people, you should know that there are a variety of beliefs and customs associated with many churches, so scope out and examine your options. There are unfortunately some churches out there that are just blatant cults and they employ many unethical methods to make you believe that they are the choice for you. Again make your selection carefully and understand the church and its beliefs.

The nine reasons for a first time visitor coming into a situation that he is unaccustomed to participating in or he feels threatened because he has no belief in God or Heaven, does not include a reference from the Bible. My reasoning is because if you assume the Bible was concocted by men who were simple minded and self-indulging and therefore has no validity in your mind, then I offer prove outside of the Bible that Heaven does exist.

1) In seeking truth, mankind has always looked for a divine reason for life. It is constantly intertwined with our history. This includes some of history's most noted scholars. A supreme being in heaven exists because he pursues us and if man was a supreme being, he would not constantly pursue celestial answers to the universe. He has always been compelled to seek hope in his searches. Mankind has always had a deep longing to find this hope outside of his realm. Life can only develop from life and it was purposely design that way. Some would state that life began as a speck of bacteria that suddenly came into being on its own. This in itself makes no sense in the continuation of life and what we know to be true. The bottom line of this fact remains that all life comes from other life.

2) We already know for a fact that unseen manifestations and indicators exist even though we physically cannot perceive these elements through our eyes. Among these existing principles are oxygen, gravity, love, dignity, pride, and yes even heaven. Anyone of these items takes a bit of faith to believe that they do exist.

Some of these principles excluding heaven took countless generations before they were considered factual. Heaven was considered a fact by many before these other principles were conceived.

3) The mere complexity of our own planet, Earth points to a deliberate design. Its position in the solar system is the perfect place for living beings. Theorists cannot comprehend that a mass of material that was flung wildly into a chaotic course would suddenly stop in a perfect orbit and obtain a life giving atmosphere. There is no case of summarized man-induced information that correctly and conclusively explains this phenomenon. Their conclusions are based on abstruse and obscure conjectures.

4) The brain of a human being was designed and created to comprehend more than any other creature on Earth. A human brain is made to create and consider other dimensions. Animals cannot conceive an idea that includes heaven, therefore a superior mind wonders about other possibilities. Mankind with his more complex cerebral cortex is the only living being on Earth that can comprehend beyond the life we have.

5) Scientists have concluded for the most part, (because they argue with their own findings) that the universe flashed into existence suddenly. They cannot come up with a valid reason of the type of force that was manufactured in creating this sudden universe. There is no comprehension theory that they have developed, let alone a mere fact that supports man's conception of the origins of the universe. Something outside of the universe caused this phenomenon because force cannot come into being without substance or another type of energy. Scientists have theories, but no positive facts that backed up their claims of what this primary force was that created our universe.

6) The universe itself operates by uniformed laws of nature. Again scientists cannot see any logical necessity for a universe that obeys rules. If a universe suddenly forms on its own, it could not exist because chaos would be the normal conclusion, but we have a universe that maintains order throughout its system. What controls this order? There is but one logical conclusion.

7) Our own DNA is made up of detailed instructions that make up a code using chemicals that instruct and construct. How can this principle operate for centuries without the intervention of mankind?

8) There is the historical and factual proof in Jesus himself, a man that the Romans crucified, but yet this individual, despite being buried for three days, was seen by many after his resurrection.

9) Finally there is mankind in general. Overall, despite ourselves, we have never been able to achieve perfection and preform unselfish love. That exists elsewhere and many believe that it does exist somewhere else. Heaven? Man, with all his assurances cannot even achieve a semblance of heaven on earth.

In many ways I believe that seeking philosophical answers to alleviate loneliness is sound and your answers could just lie in a truthful and spiritual atmosphere.

No matter the reaction, there must be a type of trepidation accompanied by loneliness because they must bear this burden alone in their mind.

What we should keep in mind is there is much about in our universe that is still beyond our understanding and that any possibility is not out of the realm of what we feel and see. Changes do exist and with that also comes the possibility of miracles and unseen breakthroughs in the field of medicine. We cannot dismiss that incidents occur of which humans cannot fully comprehend and have no account for why certain things happen. I am fully convinced that the realm of possibilities include that fact that there is always a hope in miracles.

Different theories on spiritual help

These are more examples on misconstrued speculations on the part of men that have no more clear answers then the rest us have.

When I die, I'm just a piece of meat for the worms and vultures.

I will not listen to men of wisdom who proclaimed that there is an afterlife. I am basically good and that will negate any reason to consult with anyone else who thinks they know more than I do.

There are no answers because science has not been able to prove an existence after our life here on earth.

I'm into reincarnation and I will return as a lesser being.

I can only see that the afterlife will still have different levels just like earth today.

I have no hope whatsoever of being able to go to heaven therefore I refuse any advice from men of the cloth.

All of these concepts are a manufactured creation of man's desire to be self-controlling. If we truly look deep into the recesses of the history of our species, we should state unequivocally that man is not a perfect creature, therefore we cannot assume by factual data that we are in control of our own destinies or that we are the higher link on the evolutionary scale. We are still in a learning process until the day that we depart this existence, but what we have learned should point to the fact that we are a creation that is loved and cherished.

The aftermath of death for those left behind

Take time to reminisce.

You could feel better if the memories are fond ones. Make a list of those times.

Suggestions for ideas that could possibly alleviate the indicators of loneliness

- Look at family photos or videos.
- Plant a flower or tree in memory of your special person who passed away or that you miss terribly.
- Repurpose your special person's clothing. Make pillows, quilt, teddy bear, etc.
- Have a party on your special person's birthday to celebrate life.
- Do something your special person enjoyed in their honor.
- Create something, art, poetry, song or play.
- Cook a favorite food.
- Go on a memory outing and photograph your favorite places.
- Raise money or volunteer in some way for a cause you want to support.
- Take care of the earth, clean up trash at a park, bench, or at a cemetery.
- Show kindness to someone in need such as open a door for the elderly and sick.

- Create a song list of your favorite songs. Play these songs when you experience loneliness.
- Write a letter or paint a picture.
- Visit a zoo, park or church or mall.
- Create a story.
- Come up with your own ideas.

A Recap of Some Major Points of this Book

There is a reason for the emotion of loneliness. Loneliness is an expression of a want and a change. Avoid the urge and it will return.

Loneliness can be a great motivator for connecting with others. Look for opportunities to explore and communicate with others. Be creative and come up with new ideas for sharing with others.

Use that desire and drive to come out of your depression. Loneliness means you have cerebral reasoning capacity and it is trying to tell you that a motivational change is desired and needed.

Don't ever mistake loneliness for stupidity. Extraordinary scholars and top executives experience loneliness so do not confine this malady to your own personal excuse.

Exercise as you can without over stretching your abilities. This should include limiting your television time. Take time to get out of house. Avoid overeating.

Considering exercise, I have developed a strategy that involves walking my dogs at the local dog park and meeting people at the same time. The pathway in our park is an oval in which people normally walk their pets clock-wises on the track just inside the perimeter of the park fence. I complied with that method until I realized that in breaking the usual routine and going counter clock-wises, I would see more people that were facing me. There is always someone who either smiles or greets me as I walk towards them. I might suggest that if you have a usual routine as you walk, just do the same thing, but in the opposite direction. You might just discover that you will see the same things, but with a whole new perspective.

Reflect on the times when life was perfect or near perfect. There are a number of these in each life. Think back to a time when you were extremely satisfied. A meaningful reflection of past events can be used as a motivator.

An active mind is a healthy mind. Use puzzle exercises to stimulate your senses. Check the newspaper or internet to expand your mind's stimulation.

Go back to a time that you remember when you had a best friend, a good job, and a car you could rely on. Was there a time in your life that it felt like you had no responsibilities?

Hang on to the thought but not the consequences, we all must be accountable in some way.

Remember that life is not consistent and it changes all the time. One particular bad day is not likely to remain forever. Hang on to that promise and hope, for hope springs eternal, despite the constant bombardment of a negative view of others, primarily the newscast.

Get involved. People need relationships. A person without a companion is more likely to die early in life. Look for those opportunities to make a real change in someone's life.

Expect to be a person who will have many friends, but you must willingly believe no one but yourself can solve this dilemma.

Be kind but be yourself. Do not ever give up those interests or habits that you cherish because someone else disapproves of them. I would listen if those suggested hobbies are dangerous to your well-being. If you adore stamp collecting, don't bow down to someone who wants you to give it up because he thinks it is boring.

Can be one particular indiscretion that you do not want to share with others because of the intensity of the issue at hand, but in doing so, you isolate yourself in the process because you are striving to keep your issue private.

What can actually help with loneliness?

If you or a loved one is experiencing a sense of loneliness, some simple next steps to take can be;

- Talking to friends and family.
- Even if you're not in the same city or country, a text or phone call or better still a face to face meeting will help you rekindle the sense of human connection.
- Going outside and experience the community. Have you been ordering on line and having your groceries delivered? Go out and run your own errands. The simple interaction at the store counters goes a long ways. Simply taking a walk around the block or through the park can help too in ways you can barely imagine.
- Get involved. Find a group in your community using an app. (Be not afraid of the computer!) Find sites like "MEETUP" or partner with a classmate or co-worker to organize a casual get together.

- Volunteer-Helping others is a two in one benefit and we're all about making human connections here at Crisis text line. Volunteering as a crisis counselor means being part of our big happy global family.
- Get a pet or a plant. Taking care of another living thing helps with remembering that we are all connected to one another.
- Find help if you need it.

The medical world's opinions on how to cure loneliness

1) Why not be active physically, a point that has already been made earlier in this book. Have a schedule that includes a regular workout.
2) Take some time to relax alone and meditate on your core values and principles. This does not mean sitting in front of a television. If necessary, go to a place of isolation from others and away from home.
3) Read a paper or talk to someone nearby.
4) Take care of your metabolism and physical needs when needed.
5) If loneliness is overwhelming and there is no one around to talk to, write your feelings down on paper.
6) Spend time with others. Join a club or volunteer for work. If your mind is not active, it could be detrimental to your physical well-being.
7) Learn to deal with much less of television watching and if you smoke, your chances for prolonged depression increase dramatically.
8) Maintain a healthy and constant time for your sleep period. Resting well always alleviates a sense of loneliness.

9) Acknowledge the fact that you are feeling lonely. Learn how to disengage from the feeling by trying out some of the solutions from above. This might include strangely enough, to disengage from online systems which were meant to a be a means of communication, but these devices are an ever increasing departure from what it was meant to accomplish because it allows people to not meet face to face.

10) Volunteer or join a club that you have interest. Be among those people who care about the same core values that you like and can share.

11) Practice self-care. Psychologically, we all have our wants. If we feel we cannot ever be a friend to someone, we are close to nothing. Do not entrust the view of the world that proclaims you are nothing without taking from others. Try being a true friend and scoffed at the world view, which is often flawed when it tells you that you are nothing without wealth.

What is the price of loneliness?

It depends squarely on what you do or not do if changes are to be made. The price can be too high if you succumb to the constant drudgery of an unchanging lifestyle. If you wish to maintain a life of loneliness, never try to get out of your house and take no action in a life outside of your comfort zone. If you are ready to make a new change and meet new friends, be assertive and take it upon yourself to join with others of a like mind and interest.

Be on notice that new encounters will always transform you in many varied and striking ways. Your personality could change for the better or for the worst, depending on whom you hang out with on a consistent basis. Change is inevitable in this world of ours and we change every day in appearance, thoughts and moods. Try not to be stagnant in your decision making for it will never benefit you.

There exists in the realm of human imagination the unmistakable and constant pursuit of those aspirations that we vigorously long for and want; therefore it reveals the most genuine and greatest desire that lies deep within our heart.

You can choose to avoid interaction with others and hang on to a lingering lonely life or you can facilitate boldness and take on a whole new perspective on life. You must ask the vital question; could it be that I am maintaining a lifestyle that inhibits my aspirations, or am I willing to take the appropriate steps and risks to alleviate the continued pangs of loneliness? The decision is yours to make.

You hold the answers and you must rely on your own abilities to remove the stigma of loneliness in your existence. Develop a new skill, go and reach out to people that you can relate to and create new memories. Volunteer or join an organization that caters to your hobbies and interests. In short get off your couch and explore new friendships and reconnect with old friends. It is in you to come up with the courage to alleviate your loneliness. I gave you u the information, but you can accomplish nothing without action.

For the most part your loneliness is a departure from the same old routine and it rests squarely on your shoulders. I have given you viable options. Go out and greet the world.